Copyright, Legal Notice and Disclaimer

This publication is protected under the US Copyright Act of 1976 and all other applicable international, federal, state and local laws, and all rights are reserved, including resale rights: you are not allowed to give or sell this book and the materials contained in it, to anyone else.

Please note that much of this publication is based on personal experience and anecdotal evidence. Although the author and publisher have made every reasonable attempt to achieve complete accuracy of the content in this book, they assume no responsibility for errors or omissions. Also, you should use this information as you see fit, and at your own risk. Your particular situation may not be exactly suited to the examples illustrated here; in fact, it's likely that they won't be the same, and you should adjust your use of the information and recommendations accordingly.

Any trademarks, service marks, product names or named features are assumed to be the property of their respective owners, and are used only for reference. There is no implied endorsement if I use one of these terms. All images in this book are readily available in various places on the Internet and believed to be in public domain. Images used are believed to be used within the author's and publisher's rights according to the U.S. Copyright Fair Use Act (title 17, U.S. Code.)

Finally, use your head. Nothing in this book is intended to replace common sense, legal, or other professional advice, and is meant to inform and entertain the reader.

Copyright © 2018 Sam Sommer. All rights reserved worldwide.

Introduction

If I told you that a routine trip to my favorite burger establishment consistently yielded Indian Head Pennies in the change, would you believe me? I would hand the clerk $10 for the hamburgers, fries and drink, and get back a pocket full of coins that often had Indian Heads in it. Call me a liar if you want, but I found them on a regular basis!

Do I have your attention? What I just said is true. This happened to me back in the late 1950's. It is hard to believe! Valuable coins just showed up in pocket change all the time. Collecting was not what it is today, less interest back then, and no internet. So very few knew about the value of collecting decades ago and with little competition, you could find valuable coins on a regular basis.

So if you cannot find Indian Heads today what then can you find? What do you look for and is it worth your time and effort? The best way to answer this is to first look at the behavior of my late father-in-law. He played the lottery for decades. He spent thousands upon thousands of dollars and countless hours and never had anything to show for it. Yes, he had fun and it kept his dreams alive, but what if he looked at his pocket change instead and learned which coins had value. My guess is that he would be worth a small fortune today. When you consider the money and the trips to the store to buy the tickets and if he replaced this with trips to the bank and searching through change and learning what to look for, and factor in 40 years of lotto play, my opinion is that he could have amassed a collection worth at least $500,000 today!

Believe it or not, it is as easy, if not easier, to find valuable coins in change now as it was years ago. The reason is obvious. The internet has made it really simple to learn what to look for and how much it is worth. There are all sorts of error coins in loose change and very rare (scarce) minted coins that can be found. And many have been successful doing so. One such coin found in change sold for almost $2 million dollars.

However, to make this work, you must know how to search for coins and what coins to look for. In other words, do you look at pennies, dimes, quarters, etc... and how do you get your hands on these coins in such numbers so the result pays off? Do you look for error coins and or do you look for coins that are very scarce, only a few minted? Do you buy coins and coin rolls?

I am going to answer these questions and lots more and show you exactly what to do and it won't cost you a dime. Well maybe a little gas for trips to the bank. And I will show you how I always find silver coins. In fact, I will show you one method that almost guarantees you will find silver. I will explain why you should never buy coins, especially rolls of coins from online sellers. You are going to find out what specific coins to search for so you are not wasting your time looking for a needle in a hay stack.

The secret to making this all work lies in your ability to learn exactly what coins are worth your time and effort to search for based upon the real chance of finding them and reaping the monetary benefits. And you do not need to have any experience for this to work because I am focusing on coins that are easy to spot and recognize and do not require numismatic expertise to identify. Most importantly, I will show you what to do with your coins when you find some that have value. Knowing how to sell your coins so you get the best return and do not get cheated, is critical.

This book does not attempt to list every error variety for every coin made, only ones that I believe, as stated before, you have a real chance of finding. This approach to finding valuable coins is important to take because if you were to look through a box of pennies, for example, and had a list of 200 possible error coins to look for, you would become so frustrated and so tired you would give up the searching. It would take 2-3 days to look at the 2,500 pennies and compare them to your list of 200 errors.

Chapters

Some Examples Of Valuable Finds In Loose Change?

Getting Started (Tools)

Clubs and Terminology

How To Grade Coins

How To Handle Coins

Fake Coins - Buying Safely

What Coins To Look For - Let's Start With Pennies

Jefferson Nickels

Roosevelt Dimes

Washington Quarters

Kennedy Half Dollars

Coin Roll Hunting Procedure

Finding Silver

Determining Coin Values

Selling Coins

Quick Start Guide

Conclusion and Summary

Some Examples Of Valuable Finds In Loose Change?

This is a good place to start. After all, if you have little to no faith in the chances of finding something of value, what's the point in proceeding?

In Yuma, Arizona only 155 miles from where I live in Arizona, in December of 2014, William Gaitlin, a coin enthusiast, went to the Foothills Walmart and asked the teller at the Sun Bank if they could change his $3 into pennies. Little did he know that this routine trip to Walmart to fill a prescription would make him $21,510 richer. He found a 1969 S Double Die Obverse Lincoln Penny.

I will show you what this coin looks like later. The Double Die Obverse (DDO) means that the numbering and lettering on the front of this coin was imprinted twice due to a misaligned die. Another example for this same coin occurred in 2007 when a collector purchased two rolls of pennies and found two of these coins.

Michael Tremonti also found an uncirculated 1969 S DDO while looking through a roll of pennies and because of its great condition (uncirculated – new like) it sold at auction for $126,500 in January of 2008.

A penny dated 1983 was found and after weighing, it was determined to be made out of copper rather than 97.5 % zinc. Pennies minted before 1982 were made of 95% copper. In 1982 pennies were either copper or zinc. In 1983 they were made of zinc. This find and others like it are very valuable. The penny in question sold for $23,500.

In 1999 the United Sates Mint provided General Mills with 5,500 Sacagawea dollars to promote the new coins. General Mills placed one Sacagawea dollar inside every 2000th box of Cheerios. In 2005, collector Tom Delorey discovered that some of these 5500 Sacagawea dollars bore an unusual design on the reverse. Each of the "Cheerios" dollars featured detailed veins in the eagle's tail feathers, details that were lacking on regular Uncirculated and Proof Sacagawea dollars. It is likely that the vast majority were spent by their unsuspecting owners. One coin in particular sold for almost

$10,000.

A 1992 penny was found that had lettering on the back of the coin very close together. The "AM" in the word "America" was closer than normal. Only 20 of these coins have been found. One such coin sold for over $13,000.

Another example, and one that I experienced first hand, involved my Aunt Sarah. Her late husband Joe left behind lots of coins when he passed away. Sarah knew nothing about them. My cousin asked our Aunt if he could look through them and she gave all the coins to him. He told me about the most valuable one in the lot. It was a 1916 Standing Liberty Quarter in mint condition. It had never been circulated so it looked brand new. A coin in this condition, and examples bear this out, sells for over $50,000!

Getting Started (Tools)

To make your searching easier I recommend some very basic tools. Here is a list of them and I will explain why I suggest you make these purchases.

The tools are:
- Nitrile gloves
- A jewelry loupe
- A gram scale
- A digital microscope

Nitrile gloves are used to handle coins because they are very dirty. If you look at a lot of coins in one sitting, they come in handy. You will be amazed at how dirty they get from examining coins. I also recommend that you buy powder free gloves. They come in different sizes, so order accordingly. Some people are sensitive to latex so it is best to purchase latex and powder free ones. Always order 100, you will be glad you did. They come in black and blue colors. I like the Dynarex brand found on Amazon. Sometimes Walmart carries them. Harbor Freight also has them at good prices. I usually get mine on sale at Harbor Freight for around $6.

A jewelry loupe is needed to examine coins close up. I buy them on Amazon or eBay and prefer those that have a LED light. I usually order two at a time and pay around $10 for the pair. Look for 20X or 30X power.

A gram scale is indispensable for weighing coins. These small scales are limited to 8 ounces. Certain coins need to be weighed to determine metal content, authenticity and error types. Make sure the scale you buy weighs in the 100th of a gram. Shop around on Amazon, prices and products change all the time. I use the ones from the Smart Weigh company found on Amazon for under $10. They weigh up to 2.2 kg.

Can you guess how I took this beautiful picture shown below of an 1885 Morgan

Silver Dollar? A digital microscope allows you to take great close ups of coins and jewelry. This picture shows its capability. Good quality pictures help when trying to sell an item and when trying to identify a coin. The magnification allows you to see the object close up.

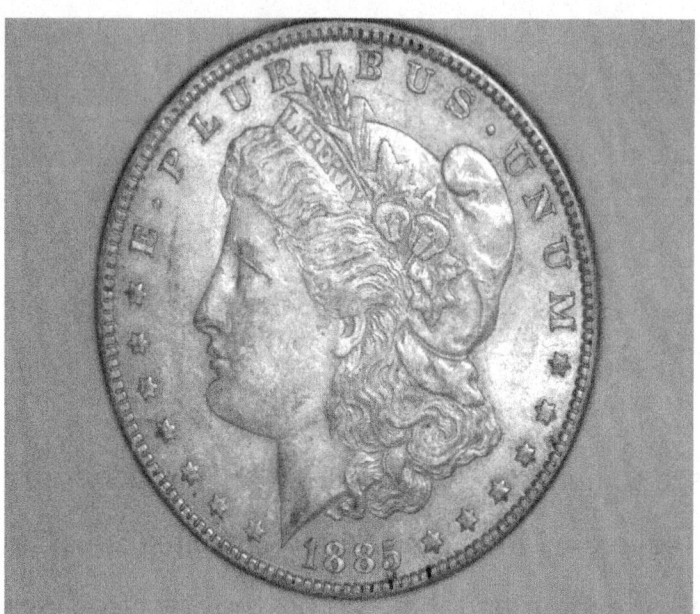

A digital microscope is an extremely valuable tool. A company called Celestron offers a great one found on Amazon for under $50. It is model #44302 and it plugs into your USB port. It will work with most computers. Check before buying.

Links to the items mentioned in this chapter as found on Amazon or eBay. If reading a paper back version of this book, I will provide the full link at book's end.

Digital Microscope

Gram Scale

Gloves

Loupe

Clubs and Terminology

Most cities and towns have a coin club. There are a number of reasons to join one, especially if you are new to coins and have children. To find local clubs in your area please contact the local chamber of commerce and the city hall. These organizations keep a directory for local businesses and organizations, like clubs.

The newspaper and local Facebook pages for your town are sources for club information. Contact them and enquire if your town has a local coin club. In addition national organizations, such as the American Numismatic Association keeps a list of clubs around the country. Search for their name or "ANA coins" to locate their website and it has links to local clubs on it.

Joining a local coin club is easy and very rewarding. They usually have a low yearly fee, mine is $16. They hold regular meetings, usually once a month and the benefits are enormous:

- They always make educational presentations – great learning resource.
- They are a great way to educate your children. Very few children participate and the members will try to help them – like helping the next generation.
- The members have hundreds of years of coin experience and can help you identify your coins.
- They routinely have auctions where you can buy coins and stamps well below market value.
- Members that you get to know will often have extra coins that they will sell to you at low prices so you can complete your collection.
- Members will buy coins from you.
- Members will have tons of resources – names of reliable dealers e.g. I routinely buy things at my coin club auctions and resell them on eBay.

Terminology is important. Let's define some terms and provide a link to a complete coin dictionary. This link is also a coin forum that is well worth joining, it is free:

http://www.coincommunity.com/dictionary/

Mintmark: A small letter(s) designating where the coin was produced.

C = Charlotte, NC (gold coins only; 1838-1861)

CC = Carson City, NV (1870-1893)

D = Dahlonega, GA (gold coins only; 1838-1861)

D = Denver, CO (1906 to date)

O = New Orleans, LA (1838-1909)

P or No Mintmark = Philadelphia, PA (1793 to date)

S = San Francisco, CA (1854 to date)

W = West Point, NY (1984 to date)

BU: Brilliant Uncirculated refers to the coins condition or grade – it is a coin that is in its original condition or mint state and has original mint luster.

Bullion/Bullion Coin: A coin (American Eagle, e.g.) or other object (bars, ingots, etc…) consisting primarily of a precious metal, e.g. silver, gold, platinum.

Business Strike: A coin minted for general circulation.

Certified: A coin that has been authenticated and graded by one of the major grading services, like: PCGS or NGS.

Circulated: Coins with obvious signs of wear due to being "circulated" in regular commerce.

Clad: Coins made from more than one layer of metal, e.g. quarters since 1965 have a pure copper core, with the outer layers copper-nickel (.750 copper, .250 nickel).

Grade or Grading: A term used to define the coins condition.

Key/Key Date: Refers to the scarcest coins in a series and carries a higher price, e.g. 1909-S VDB Lincoln Cent which is the rarest coin in the Lincoln Penny series.

Luster: The brilliance or shine of a coin and is considered to be one of the main factors in the coins value and grade.

Mint Set: An official set containing one uncirculated coin for each denomination made that year.

MS/Mint State: A term to describe a coin in the condition as it left the mint, uncirculated coins or BU.

NGC: Numismatic Guaranty Corporation is one of the major grading companies.

Numismatics: The study, art or collection of coins, medals, tokens and similar objects.

Numismatist: A person who is knowledgeable in the collecting of coins, medals, tokens and similar objects.

Patina: A term used to describe the lighter shades of toning on a coin.

PCGS: Professional Coin Grading Service is one of the major grading companies.

Proof: A specially produced coin made from highly polished planchets and dies and often struck more than once to accent the design. Proof coins receive the highest quality strike possible and can be distinguished by their sharpness of detail and brilliant, mirror-like surface and sometimes cameo effect.

Proof Set: A complete set of proof coins for each denomination made that year and specially packaged.

Relief: The part of a coin's design that is raised above the surface.

Reverse: The back of the coin or tails.

Rim: The raised outer edge of the coin, that helps protect the design from wear.

Slab: A nickname referring to coins that have been graded by a third party service and placed in a plastic holder.

Strike: The act of impressing the image on to the planchet. The quality of the strike is an important part of the grading process.

Toning: Coloring on the surface of a coin caused by a chemical reaction, such as sulfur from older cardboard books, flips or envelopes. Rainbow-colored toning and original toning is often a desirable characteristic to many collectors.

Type Set: A collection of one coin for each denomination and/or a particular design.

Ask Price: The selling price a dealer offers.

Bid Price: The price a dealer pays for bullion or coins.

Bullion: Precious metals like platinum, gold or silver in the form of bars or other storage shapes. Bullion coins are made of these metals, too.

Collector Coin, Historic Coin, or Numismatic Coin: A coin whose value is based on rarity, demand, condition, and mintage; in fact, it may be worth more than its bullion value.

Melt Value: The basic intrinsic bullion value of a coin if it were melted and sold.

Premium: The amount by which the market value of a gold coin or bar exceeds the actual value of its gold content. The seller can recover part of the premium at resale.

Spot Price: The current price in the physical market for immediate delivery; sometimes called the cash price.

Spread: The difference between the buying price and the selling price.

Troy Ounce: The unit of weight for precious metals. One troy ounce equals 480 grains, 1.09711 ounces, or 31.103 grams.

One of the best ways to learn about coins is by joining a forum. We mentioned one earlier, here are some more:

CoinTalk Forums: https://www.cointalk.com/forums/ These forums are perfect for beginning coin collectors and expert coin collectors. I really love the community here.

Susan Headley's Coin Forum: Susan Headley is one of the best coin bloggers. She writes the Susan's Coins Blog at About.com. If you have not read Susan's blog articles, head on over there right now. She is an excellent writer and very passionate about coins. In addition to being a great writer, Susan has a great coin collecting forum.

Collector's Universe Forums: Collector's Universe does not just cater to coin collectors. However, this forum does have an active coin collector community.

Another great forum: www.Coinpeople.com

How To Grade Coins

When you look for coins of value you will notice that the condition of the money you handle varies. Some coins are bright and shinny, almost new, and others are worn down. The point of this chapter is to introduce you to the concept of coin grading or deciding what condition a coin is in. For purposes of this book you should only be familiar with the concept and not worry about grading a coin yourself. That's where the experts come in and I will show you how to get your coins graded later.

The reason grading is so important has to do with the value a coin has. The better it's condition or grade, the more value it has. Keep in mind that new coins have a high grade because they were freshly minted and not handled much. However, that does not make them worth more than another new coin that is worn down. The grading plays a key role when a coin has some value to begin with and then the higher grade drives the price up. This is the general rule but keep in mind that there are exceptions to this rule, but don't worry about it for now. It does not affect your coin hunting in any way.

Let's look at an example. Suppose you find a 2017 penny that looks brand new and it happens to have a major error on it. Let's say the date is doubled. You set it aside and do some research and find that only 5 of these coins have been found so far. You read that one of them just sold for $10,000 and it was mint like or brand new looking. The coin you found is new looking, very shinny also, but has a major scratch on it. Your coin, because of the mark, may only bring in $1,000.

The 1916 Standing Liberty Quarter I mentioned earlier that was worth over $50,000 because it was in a mint state or new, may only be worth $1,000 if it is worn down.

There is a standard that has been developed to help us decide what the condition or grade is. On a 70-point grading scale coins are assigned a numeric value. It is called the Sheldon Scale. The Sheldon Scale ranges from a grade of Poor (P-1) to Perfect Mint State (MS-70.) Grades are usually assigned at key points on this scale, with the most commonly used points being: (Information from about.com)

(P-1) Poor - Barely identifiable; must have date and mintmark, otherwise pretty thrashed.

(FR-2) Fair - Worn almost smooth but lacking the damage Poor coins have.

(G-4) Good - Heavily worn such that inscriptions merge into the rims in places; details are mostly gone.

(VG-8) Very Good - Very worn, but all major design elements are clear, if faint. Little if any central detail.

(F-12) Fine - Very worn, but wear is even and overall design elements stand out boldly. Almost fully-separated rims.

(VF-20) Very Fine - Moderately worn, with some finer details remaining. All letters of LIBERTY, (if present,) should be readable. Full, clean rims.

(EF-40) Extremely Fine - Lightly worn; all devices are clear, major devices bold.

(AU-50) About Uncirculated - Slight traces of wear on high points; may have contact marks and little eye appeal.

(AU-58) Very Choice About Uncirculated - - Slightest hints of wear marks, no major contact marks, almost full luster, and positive eye appeal.

(MS-60) Mint State Basal - Strictly uncirculated but that's all; ugly coin with no luster, obvious contact marks, etc.

(MS-63) Mint State Acceptable - Uncirculated, but with contact marks and nicks, slightly impaired luster, overall basically appealing appearance. Strike is average to weak.

(MS-65) Mint State Choice - Uncirculated with strong luster, very few contact marks, excellent eye appeal. Strike is above average.

(MS-68) Mint State Premium Quality - Uncirculated with perfect luster, no visible contact marks to the naked eye, exceptional eye appeal. Strike is sharp and attractive.

(MS-69) Mint State All-But-Perfect - Uncirculated with perfect luster, sharp, attractive strike, and very exceptional eye appeal. A perfect coin except for microscopic flaws (under 8x magnification) in planchet, strike, or contact marks.

(MS-70) Mint State Perfect - The perfect coin. There are no microscopic flaws visible to 8x, the strike is sharp, perfectly-centered, and on a flawless planchet. Bright, full, original luster and outstanding eye appeal.

A simplified version may be more helpful:

Prefix	Numerical Grade	Description
MS	60–70	Mint State (Uncirculated)
AU	50, 53, 55, 58	About Uncirculated
XF	40, 45	Extremely Fine
VF	20, 25, 30, 35	Very Fine
F	12, 15	Fine
VG	8, 10	Very Good
G	4, 6	Good
AG	3	About Good
FA	2	Fair
PR	1	Poor

Just be aware of the fact that grading is a key variable when determining value. Do not try to grade a coin yourself. If you find a valuable coin I will tell you how to have it graded professionally. The small fee you pay for this service will pay off in the end.

How To Handle Coins

Knowing how to handle coins properly is important. Coins are dirty, so wearing gloves helps. Handling valuable coins and special coins should be spoken about. Some coins can be damaged just by breathing on them, and some can be damaged by touching them. This results in lowering their value. Valuable coins should never be cleaned by you, only by professionals.

Years ago coin holders were not properly made and coins became damaged when stored in them. This problem has been corrected today. The chemical in the holder (usually a card board holder) reacted with the coin, producing a discoloring of the coin or a toning of the coin. Toned coins can have value. The reason I mention this subject is due to the fact that you may come across a very valuable coin and you should only handle it with cotton gloves to maintain its value, no cleaning. Please note: a valuable coin after improper cleaning can be reduced in worth by 90%.

Common coins can be cleaned with soap and water, but no abrasive material or cleanser should be used. Use your fingers to soak the coin in soap and water, do one coin at a time. Rub the coin with your fingers, then rinse the soap and water off with distilled water then place the coin on a towel to dry (don't use your nails).

Because you may come across a toned or sometimes called rainbow toned coin, it is important to examine this subject. Coins react to chemicals around them, either by touch or by exposure through the air. Believe it or not some toned or rainbow toned coins actually are more valuable than plain coins. It depends on the coin and how they look.

If you come across a valuable coin set it aside and place it in a plastic bag until it can be professionally graded.

Here's a picture of a toned 1941 penny that is worth thousands of dollars because of it's incredible toning and the condition it is in. It is hard to find coins like this but be aware that they exist. If you find one set it aside.

PCGS
The Standard for the Rare Coin Industry

Certificate No.
11747096
Verify the authenticity of this image at PCGS.com

Fake Coins – Buying Safely

I do not recommend that you ever buy coins online unless you are a very seasoned collector. The FBI states that over 50% of the coins sold online are fake! This rule also applies to rolls of coins sold online. What you will learn in this book is the proper way to get your hands on large numbers of coins so you can search through them and look for gems. Let's examine the problems relating to buying rolls of coins online, especially on eBay: Almost all the rolls on eBay are fake. They have been manipulated by the seller to appear in such a way that the buyer is tempted to buy or bid because of the end coins that have some value. How is this done?

It is very simple. Just buy a coin crimping machine and some old looking wrappers and put a few Indian Head Pennies at each end and you are in business. Here's a machine on Amazon that can make big money if you are unethical.

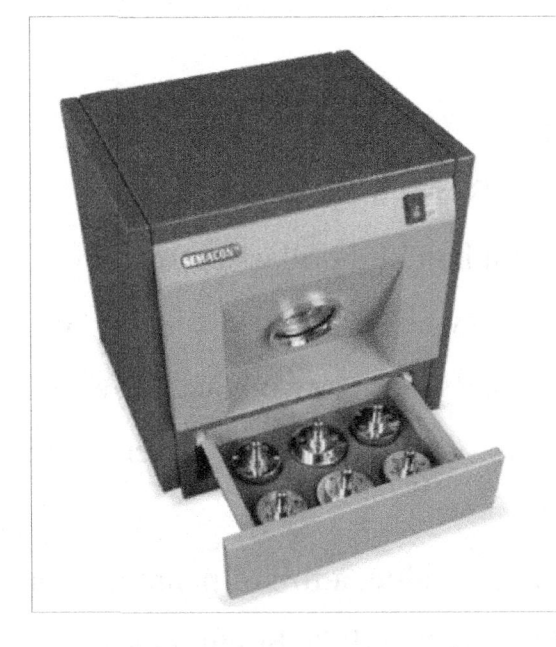

Semacon CM-75 Coin Roll Wrapper Crimping Machine (Crimper) w/ 6 Heads
by Semacon
Be the first to review this item

List Price: $775.00
Price: $706.88 + $42.75 shipping
You Save: $68.12 (9%)

In stock.
Usually ships within 2 to 3 days.
Ships from and sold by Sale Stores.

- Safe, you can touch the rotating head while it's spinning and it won't hurt you.
- Requires only a couple of seconds to proficiently seal coin wrappers.
- Includes the following crimping heads: 1¢, 5¢, 10¢, 25¢, 50¢, $1 (SBA/Golden)
- Includes a crimp head storage drawer.

2 new from $700.20

Buying unsearched rolls:

A great article from eBay illustrates my point:

At any given time, eBay has a few hundred auctions for unsearched rolls. The new fad on eBay is bank wrapped rolls showing a key or semi-key date on the end, and the old fad is pointing to their (the seller's) feedback on how many key dates that have been found in the rolls they are selling. Most coins found in bank wrapped rolls are common and well circulated coins. Shot gun wrapped rolls can be opened, searched, then re-crimped as if it came from a bank. The same rolls can be searched and a key date put on the end, then re-crimped as unsearched.

For example, let's say I have a shot gun roll of Lincoln Wheat Cents, and all are common dates. So, I buy a 1909-S (The "S" means it was minted in San Francisco) key date for $125, (this is the actual book value of the coin in good condition), and I replace the end coin with the 1909-S Lincoln. Also, I know that a 1909-S with the VDB on the back is worth $900, and I also know that you can't see if the 1909-S on the end of the re-crimped roll has a VDB or not. Now I start my auction on eBay with a statement "Unsearched shotgun roll with a 1909-S showing", and a question "Is this a 1909-S VDB?".

I sit back and watch my $125 investment sell for over $255.00 because some buyers wanted to risk the chance to discover a 1909-S VDB. So, they pay $130 more than the roll is worth, and my Paypal account grows over a hundred dollars more. Now I'm thinking, "What if I did this with 10 rolls? I could make well over a thousand dollars in a week!" To top it all off, other eBay sellers see my success and copy my act. Now, it's a huge problem. Don't get into "lottery" wars like this with other bidders. It's never worth it!

Let's look at one of these tempting eBay rolls: Unbelievable, a roll of pennies with an Indian Head at one end probably worth $2 is selling for $42, and the bidding hasn't ended yet.

Look at the seller's feedback below, yet people are still bidding:

To sum up I urge you not to buy coins online unless you have years of experience. Do not buy rolls of coins online. You can get them at your local bank for free.

What Coins To Look For – Let's Start With Pennies

Now the fun begins! As I said before in order to be successful at coin hunting, you must know what to look for and the coins searched for must be easy to recognize and the chances of finding them must be great. Some of the coins I will list will be easy to find and some harder to locate. In a future chapter I will explain how to get your hands on lots of change so you can play the numbers game. The more coins you search the better your chances of success.

First let's take a look at coin denominations. The obvious question is, which coin type will yield the greatest success? The answer is simple, the Lincoln Penny. It was first minted in 1909 and still being made today. There are more valuable pennies in change than any other coin type. However, I will also look at nickles, dimes, quarters and half dollars because there are some key dates that have value and they can be found. I will provide a list for all these coins in an easy to use format in the appendix for handy reference. I will also show you how to determine a coins value.

Please note that pennies are minted in Philadelphia, Denver and San Francisco.

Pennies from Philadelphia have no mint mark on them except in 2017, when the letter "P" appears under the date. Coins from Denver have a "D" under the date. Coins made in San Francisco have an "S" under the date. So if I refer to a particular penny by its year but make no mention of "D" or "S" you know that you are looking for a coin minted in Philadelphia that has no letter under the date. And if I state a year and "D" it means minted in Denver and the "D" will be seen under the date. The same holds true for "S" or San Francisco coins.

Let's start by looking at the most valuable penny in existence. It is almost impossible to find one but you should be aware that more exist. According to the American Numismatic Association, the 1943 copper alloy cent is one of the most idealized and potentially one of the most sought after items in American numismatics. Nearly all circulating pennies at that time were struck in zinc coated steel because copper and nickel were needed for the Allied war effort.

Approximately 40 1943 (No mint mark) copper alloy cents are known to remain in existence. Coin experts speculate that they were struck by accident when copper alloy 1 cent blanks remained in the press hopper when production began on the new steel pennies.

One such coin sold for 1.7 million dollars in 2010. It was the only 1943 "D" minted copper coin ever found. The D means it was minted in Denver. Many fakes exist so be aware of this fact. Pennies minted in 1943 were made of steel and do not look like normal copper pennies:

A copper penny on the left vs a steel penny on the right:

The 1969 "S" Double Die Obverse Lincoln Cent mentioned earlier is a very valuable coin that climbs in value each year. Approximately 35 of these coins have been found in change. No doubt many more exist. With one coin in mint condition selling for $126,500 the search continues. The coin is easy to spot because it has strong doubling on all letters and numbers on the *front* or *obverse* side of the coin.

A true double die coin can be confused with a coin that has another form of doubling which occurs when the coin or the machine making the coin, shifts. What you end up with are two images of the date and or lettering but it is easy to tell the real double die from the strike(machine) double by the way it looks. Strike doubling has no value. One of the features of strike doubling is the very flat nature of the doubling vs a more whole and rounded doubling on the true and valuable double die.

Notice this coin shown below. The date and "S" that lie flat on the coin surface appear to be flat. In other words, the first strike is flat looking. This coin has no value and is a strike doubled coin or mechanical doubled coin:

An actual 1969 S double die obverse penny does not look flat. Both images of the date and the "S" are raised and rounded. On a double die obverse 1969 S Penny all the numbers and letters on the front of the coin are doubled, not just the date:

Notice the coin below how the date and the letter "S" under the date is rounded and the date closest to the coin surface is not flat looking. This is an image of a true DDO 1969 S penny. The doubling is found on all the numbers and letters on the front of the coin not just the date.

Another penny of interest is the 1992 (No mint mark) Close "AM". Approximately 10 of these coins have been found with the record sale over $25,000. The next image shows how the lettering in the word America (the second image) on the reverse side of the coin has the letters "AM" very close together. Pennies produced in 1992 had the letters much further apart (the first image) but some, by mistake, had the lettering close. This close design was intended for coins minted in 1993, not 1992.

The same thing happened for pennies minted in Denver of that year. The 1992 "D" for Denver penny was mistakenly minted with the "AM" too close together. Approximately 20 of these coins have been found with one auction bringing in over $14,000.

The 1972 (No mint mark) DDO Penny is similar to the 1969 S Double Die Obverse. This particular error is fairly easy to find and approximately 10,000 have been uncovered. The record auction price for one in extremely good condition was almost $13,000. Notice the nice doubling on the coin's front in the image below:

Please note that there are many types of 1972 DDO coins. Some have complete doubling on the entire front, others have partial or less complete doubling. Any form of doubling on the front of a 1972 penny should be set aside for further evaluation.

Another rare and hard to find coin is the 1964 (No mint mark) penny that was minted with a special finish on it. This special look or finish was intended for coins minted in 1965 mint sets. The 2 to 3 dozen found so far illustrates how rare it is. Look for a 1964 very shinny penny that has a different looking surface to it. With one selling for over $11,000 it is worth searching for. If you find a 1964 coin with what appears to be a very different surface look, set it aside for evaluation.

The 1983 (No mint mark) DDR or Double Die Reverse has nice doubling on the back side lettering. With about 5000 found so far your chances of success are high. You will be motivated to look for them because one in a high grade sold for over $7,000.

The 1984 (No mint mark) DDO or Double Die Front has some unusual doubling and one coin sold for over $3,000. The doubling shows up on the ear and chin:

The 1995 (No mint mark) DDO or Double Die Obverse (Front) has some doubling and it is not quite as clear as other DDO pennies. Even though 40,000 have been found, the record sale is over $5,000. The next image shows the subtle doubling:

The 1970 "S" Large Date DDO is another valuable and rare coin worth looking for. The record sale is over $24,000. The doubling on the words "In God We Trust" is very noticeable. Only about 50 have been found so far. Now let's look at the large date vs the small date so you know the difference between the two. The top of the 7 in the large date is below the top of the 0 and the bottom of the 7 is below the bottom of the 0:

LARGE DATE   **SMALL DATE**

The 1970 S Small Date Penny, because fewer of these were made when compared to the large date 1970 S, is worth looking for and keeping, if you find one in very good condition. The record sale for this coin in an ultra high grade is almost $2,500.

The 1982 (No mint mark) DDR is an example of a penny that does not receive much attention, probably because only three have been found. All the lettering on the reverse side of this coin is doubled. It is believed that many more exist. Why not look at the back of all 1982 pennies for this DDR (Double Die Reverse). It is hard to price this coin because as you will learn the numismatic marketplace is a strange environment. If a collector wants a coin and has the money they will pay whatever it takes to get it. On the other hand, you may have unique coin, only one exists, and it may sell for much less than you imagined it would. The reason is simple. Collectors don't want it that badly even though it is rare. More on this subject later.

In 1983, besides the DDR, mentioned earlier, another error occurred. It is referred to as "extra letters in the motto". It is believed that the die had picked up extra metal and when it struck the penny placed a line on it. The picture below shows that extra metal line and it shows the partial extra letter "G":

When looking at 1983 pennies, you should also weigh them. If one weighs 3.1 grams, you have found a copper penny. All 1983 pennies were made of zinc and weigh 2.5 grams. A few however by mistake were made of copper. They are extremely valuable and can fetch over $20,000.

In 1999 (No mint mark) some pennies minted had the "AM" lettering on the back of the coin far apart, instead of close together. This coin is referred to as the wide AM and one coin in a high grade sold for $2,300. Only about 2,500 of this penny type have been found.

In 1988 for both the plain (No Mint Mark -Philadelphia minted) penny and the "D" for Denver minted penny the designer initials exhibited errors on some coins. It is referred to as Bold Lettering instead of the thinner lettering. Frank Gasparo designed the reverse side of the Lincoln cent used from 1959 – 2008. His letters "FG" appear on the rear of the coin near the right side of the columns. This bold lettering is a mistake. It was intended for 1989 coins. The 1988 D bold lettering coin is harder to find.

Here is what the lettering looks like. The bold FG, first image, has a serif on the G. It is the extra metal that points back (the vertical line on the G) and the bold FG is closer to the base of the monument:

Jefferson Nickels

Nickels are like the forgotten child. They are part of the family but no one pays much attention to them. However, once you become familiar with the Jefferson Nickel you quickly realize that collecting them and looking for their errors is well worth the time and effort. In fact, if you are new to coins, starting your collection with nickel hunting and buying is the easiest and fastest way to gain insight and confidence in your collecting abilities. And, as we will examine in this chapter, can pay off in a big way because there are some good nickel errors that are fairly easy to find.

The Jefferson Nickel was first minted in 1938, taking the place of the Buffalo Nickel. It is still being made today. It should be pointed out that aged nickels are fairly easy to find when you look through coin rolls and often show up in very good condition. Older nickels in very excellent condition are worth a premium. Nickels tend to wear down quickly, yet many people hoard them, accounting for the new looking coins that you can sometimes find. All aged coins in great condition should be saved for further analysis. Nickels minted from 1942-1945 had 35% silver in them and should also be kept. Some 1942 nickels are not silver. The silver ones have a large "P" or "S" above the Monticello dome.

Here are some specifics regarding mint mark location and metal value:

It is important to know about the metal composition of nickels because at times they are worth a lot more than 5 cents. A standard nickel is 25% nickel and 75% copper. **"War Nickels"** (mid-1942 to 1945) are 56% copper, 35% silver, and 9% manganese. Silver nickels contain 0.05626 troy ounces of silver.

When the price of copper and or nickel rises the actual value of a nickel is more than 5 cents. When this happens people hoard them for resale. All wartime nickels are worth more than 5 cents because of their silver content. The web site coinflation shows them to be worth $.96 each (Jan 2018).

http://www.coinflation.com/silver_coin_values.html

Wartime silver nickels (1942-1945) have a mint mark above the dome, see the letter "P" below. It could be an "S" for San Francisco or a "P" for Philadelphia, the cities that minted the coins. Denver minted coins had no silver in them for the year 1942 but did contain silver for 1943, 1944 and 1945. All nickels minted with dates 1943-1945 have silver in them.

In order to properly identify your Jefferson Nickels that you find it is important to know where the mint marks or letters indicating where the coins were made are located. It can be confusing.

Located from 1938 to 1964 to the right of Monticello, except for "wartime nickels" which have a large mint mark above Monticello shown above (no mint marks used from 1965 to 1967).

From 1968 to 2004, slightly clockwise from the last digit of the date.

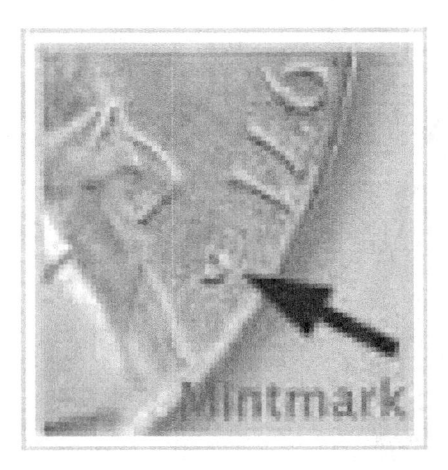

In 2005, under "Liberty".

Since 2006, under the date. Philadelphia Mint specimens before 1980 lack a mint mark, except for wartime nickels, which have a P for Philadelphia, if struck there.

The Speared Bison

In 2005, the U.S. Mint resurrected the bison reverse design on the Jefferson nickel. That same year, there were several coins discovered which contained a large die gouge. These coins were minted in Denver and have the letter "D" under the date. The die gouge is very noticeable and it can easily be seen running through the bison's back. It is not known how many of these coins were made. The top sale to date exceeds $1,000. Coins in very good condition are harder to find because the planchets used to make the coins were imperfect. In 2005 two types of nickels were minted – one with the Bison on the reverse and one with an ocean on the reverse. You will notice that when you look at large numbers of nickels you will come across many 2005 Bison coins and the spear is very noticeable on the error coin shown below:

In 1939 (No mint mark) the Mint produced an unknown number of DDR or Double Die Reverse coins. There are 2 types worth noting. One is the DDR where the letters "OF AMERICA, UNITED STATES, and CENTS" had strong doubling. This type of DDR is somewhat common and not worth as much as the DDR "MONTICELLO". The DDR 1939 nickle of this type had strong doubling in the letters of "MONTICELLO and FIVE CENTS". One such coin in a high grade sold for over $20,000. Here is a picture of it shown below:

In 1943, a wartime silver nickel error had doubling on the front of the coin. Only the coins minted in Philadelphia had this error. The letter "P" shows up above the Monticello located on the reverse side, indicating that it was made in Philadelphia. This DDO nickel has a record sale of over $11,000. Coin error is pictured below:

Ironically, 1943 "P" Silver Nickels had another type of error. It is referred to as the 3 over 2 error. The number "3" has a number "2" below it. It is hard to spot but with the record sale over $16,000 it is worth the effort:

In 1945 some nickels minted in Philadelphia exhibited doubling on the reverse side. These DDR coins also had doubling on the word "MONTICELLO" and "Five Cents" as did the 1939 nickel mentioned earlier. Look for strong doubling on the letters "C,E,L,L,O" in Monticello and "E,S" in the word cents. One such coin sold for over $14,000.

In 1946 some coins minted in San Francisco exhibited doubling in the date and on the letters in the word "Liberty", particularly the letters "B,E,R,T and Y". Their value depends upon condition. One such coin sold for over $1100. The "S" mint mark appears on the back of the coin on the right side of the Monticello building.

In 1954 some nickels from the Denver mint ("D" located to the right of the Monticello building) had strong doubling on the reverse side. The letters in the Latin words "Pluribus and Unum" exhibit this trait. DDR errors occurred again in 1956 from Denver, 1959 from Denver, 1962 from Denver, 1964 from Denver. All of these coins have some value but do not command premium prices.

In 2004 some nickels from Philadelphia had doubling on the front. The date and the letters in the word "Trust" exhibit this trait. This coin error does not draw much attention. The record sale is over $300. The letter "P" is next to the last digit on the date.

Roosevelt Dimes

In 1946 the U. S. Mint produced the first Roosevelt Dime. The Mercury Dime it replaced was made of 90% silver. Ironically some of the first Roosevelt Dimes minted were made of silver, and examples have been found for 1965 and 1966 coins. Besides a silvery appearance, which veteran coin enthusiasts easily spot, these silver dimes weigh 2.5 grams instead of 2.27 grams. Please note that unless you are a highly seasoned numismatic expert, do not use color or the silvery shade to gauge metal content. I have seen numerous silver coins that were very dirty and lacked any silver appearance yet contained 90% silver. This rule applies to any type of silver coin. Use weight as your judge.

While only about two dozen silver 1965 and 1966 coins have ever been found, take a few seconds and weigh any 1965 and 1966 dimes you come across because the $10,000 or more value they have makes this extra step worthwhile.

Another anomaly occurred when in 1982 the U. S. Mint in Philadelphia forgot to place a letter "P" on top of the date indicating where the coin was made. To help clarify mint mark existences and location:

The letter "P" appears on all Philadelphia coins minted from 1980 – present. From 1946 – 1979 no "P" was used.

"D" for Denver coins were made starting in 1946 – present. However from 1965-1967 no "D" was used.

The letter "S" appears on coins minted from 1946-1955. From 1965-present the letter "S" was only used for coins put into specials sets but can be found in change now and then.

These 1982 no "P" dimes were minted in great quantity until the mistake was noticed and then corrected. Look for these no "P" dimes because the record sale is over $2,000. Jaime Hernandez, the price guide editor for the coin grading company, PCGS tells the whole story as found on the PCGS web site and it is worth quoting because it is a fabulous read:

"The 1982 No P Dime is the first U.S. business strike coin which accidentally left the U.S. Mint, without containing its intended mint mark. Because of the missing mint mark, this coin is now worth hundreds of times more than its original face value.

The 1982 No P Dimes were originally discovered on December of 1982. Most of the coins were initially found in Sandusky Ohio, where approximately 8,000 to 10,000 coins were reportedly found. Many more 1982 No P Dimes were also handed out at the local Cedar Point Amusement Park as change, with additional examples also being found in circulation around the same area. Walter Placzwkis, Andrew Macdonald and Lane Durkee were some of three first individuals who were credited with discovering the coins.

Coincidentally, there were two different varieties discovered for the 1982 No P Dimes. The first being the sharply struck examples, while the second variety displayed a much weaker strike.

In Walter Breen's Encyclopedia of U. S. Coins, he mentions a prominent dealer from Toledo who managed to single handedly purchase over 1,500 examples of the 1982 No P Dimes when they were originally discovered, but the book doesn't mention the dealer's name. However, in 2007 I had the opportunity to speak with Clyde Englehardt from Toledo Coin Exchange, this is the dealer whom Walter Breen is referring too in his book.

Clyde who has been a full time coin dealer since 1960 told me about the 1982 No P Dimes in a very detailed conversation. Clyde says he still remembers the time when the coins were first being discovered and how some of the local dealers were offering him the coins in large quantities, including the local bank tellers who were also offering the coins to him by the roll. Clyde also mentioned that he was only able to place 47 to 48 sharply struck 1982 No P Dimes in a roll, while being able to place 50 or 51 of the weakly struck varieties inside a roll, since the sharply struck examples were thicker than the weaker struck varieties.

Clyde also mentions that he never found a single example of the 1982 No P Dime in circulation, even though he was in the area where most of the coins were being found. Nonetheless, he is very happy that he had the opportunity to purchase many of the 1982 No P Dimes when they were first being discovered. Additionally, this was a very exciting time in the coin hobby, and for him to be in the mix of it all, only made it much more exciting. Clyde later donated examples of the 1982 No Dimes to the Smithsonian Institution and the ANA.

Furthermore, in 1982 the expected die life of a Roosevelt dime die was somewhere around 75,000 coins being struck per each pair of dies. Since, there is a Strong and a Weak variety known from two different dies, it is estimated that no more than 150,000 of these coins exist. PCGS has graded just over 2,000 of both the 1982 No P Dime varieties and keep in mind, Clyde handled over 1,500 coins alone. This means that there are probably many more coins somewhere out there just waiting to be found.

Since the 1982 No P Dimes were being found in circulation, they brought a lot of attention to the coin hobby when they were originally discovered. In return, many people became coin collectors by trying to find these coins in circulation, where many of these individuals couldn't believe that the coins were worth a premium due to the missing details or mint mark, (especially since this is very uncommon in most other markets). In fact, out of all the markets in the entire world, it is very difficult to find a market such as the coin market, where an item is desired more because the item is missing certain details. The 1982 No P Dime is just one prime example of many other coins which command huge premiums in the coin market because it lacks certain details.

Finally, the 1982 No P Dime is a special coin in numismatics, since it was the first and still remains as the only business strike coin which left the U.S. Mint, without containing its intended mint mark on the obverse side of the coin."

You never know what can happen when the government does something and when you consider how many billions of coins are made each year who knows what strange errors might show up.

There are a number of Roosevelt Dime errors to be on the lookout for in addition to the silver dimes and the 1982 no "P" dime.

In 1974 Denver minted dimes were produced that had a counter clash on them. The number made and their worth is being debated. Suffice it to say that one in good condition may fetch many thousands of dollars. Counter clashes are a form of die clash that leaves part of design element or at times a full design element transferred to another part of the die. In other words, part of the front of the coin may show up on the back side and vice versa. In the case of the 1974 "D" clash the front shows up on the back and is very noticeable. Notice the outline of the flat head (upside down) of Roosevelt showing up on the back of this dime – the arrow points to his mouth:

There are a number of Double Die varieties for the Roosevelt Dime series. Many of them are hard to spot, especially for the beginner. However, I will mention some of them. The 1967 DDO coin is very rare and only several have been found. The doubling occurs in the motto "In God We Trust" and in the designer initials "JS" which appears under the neck to the right. This coin in good condition may result in thousands of dollars at auction.

Again in 1968 doubling shows up on the date, initials and the lettering on the front of the coin. Strong doubling occurs in the word "Liberty". It can bring over $150 when sold but is considered a minor variety. Again the 1970 P dime has strong doubling on the reverse (DDR). Not much value here, maybe $75. The 1970 D DDR has doubling on the words "United" and "States". Might fetch $75 if in good condition. Another variety for this coin shows doubling of the letters in "OF" and "America". It has little worth.

Washington Quarters

The George Washington Quarter was first minted in 1932. From 1932 until 1964 they were made of 90% silver. From 1965 – Present they are 75% copper and 25% nickel. The mint marks are located as follows:

Washington Quarter Mint Mark Locations

Since 1968   1932 - 1964

Mint Mark

Mint Mark

During the first few years of production the U. S. Mint mistakenly used the wrong stock metal to make quarters. This resulted in very thin coins that had the thickness of a dime rather than a quarter. These coins have been found for 1965, 1967, 1970-D, 1979 quarters and their value in good condition can exceed $100. Simply handle any quarter from these years and you can feel how thin they are. Wrong stock coins dated 1970-D were minted in abundance and can easily be found.

Another stock error resulted in a few 1965 and 1968-S quarters being minted of silver by mistake. A normal quarter weighs 5.67 grams. Any 1965 or 1968-S quarter that weighs 6.25 grams or looks silvery in appearance can yield you a $5,000 or more bonus.

Perhaps the most noted quarter error occurred in 2004 when Denver minted quarters had an extra leaf show up on some coins. Referred to as the high leaf for one type and the low leaf for another, these error coins have drawn a great deal of attention and for those lucky enough to find one can put an extra bundle of money in your pocket. Look at the reverse side corn husk for all 2004-D coins you come across

The record sale for the high leaf coin is around $2500 and for the low leaf it is $3500. This picture shows the extra leaf:

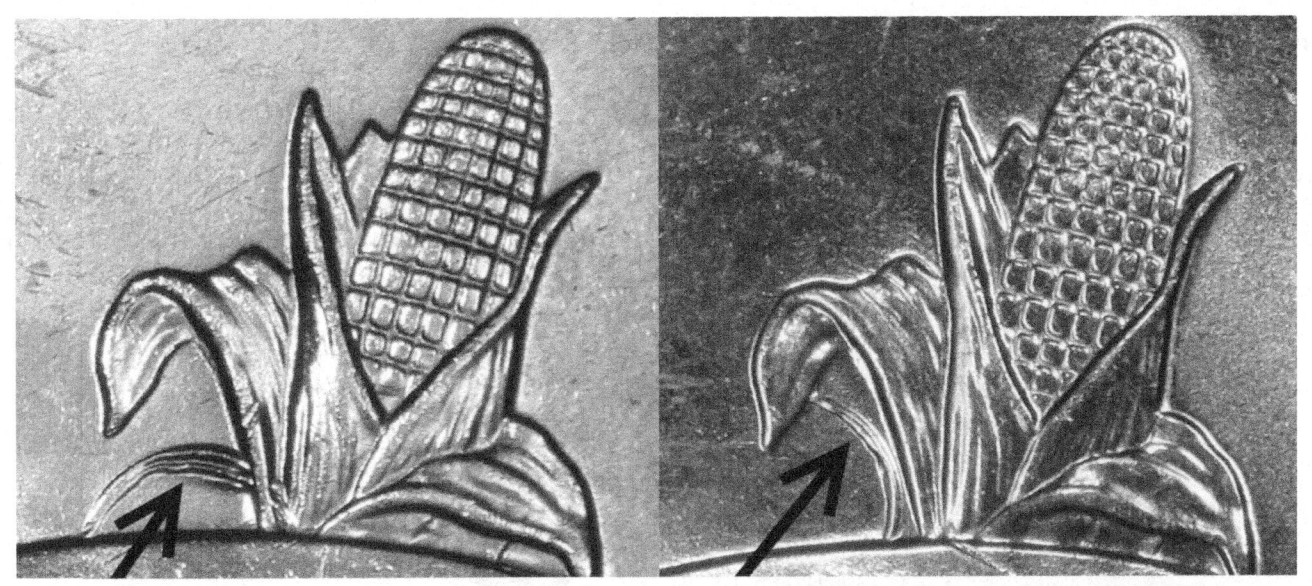

EXTRA LEAF LOW   **EXTRA LEAF HIGH**

For 1999 – P&D quarters a second or duplication of the word "Rodney" appears under the name Caesar Rodney. This counter clash is hard to find and may be worth many thousands.

A number of DDO or double die obverse quarters have been found. In 1965 a DDO occurred and is worth many thousands in good condition. Look for letter doubling in the phrase "In God We Trust" and in the word "Liberty". In 1970 some Denver minted coins had doubling in the phrase "In God We Trust" and in the date. It can easily bring in over $1000 in mint condition. Again in 1976 for Denver coins this DDO quarter has strong doubling in the word "Liberty" and is worth over $1000 in mint condition. There are many other types of DDO quarters but they are very hard to spot because of their subtleness. In other words they are hard to see.

Several good DDR or double die reverse coins have been found. The 1968-D quarter has bold doubling on the entire back of the coin and has a record sale of over $1500. Again in 1971 very thick letters can be found in the words "United States" and in the rest of the reverse. The record sale is over $9000. The 1971-D coin also has this doubling on the reverse and can be seen in the phrase "United States of America". It can easily bring in over $500.

In 2009 quarters from the Philadelphia mint exhibited some doubling of letters on the reverse side. Under the name "Duke Ellington" a second set of letters "ELL" show up on the error coins. It is hard to estimate value but in good condition they may bring in $500 or more. A recent sale one eBay went or $750.

Kennedy Half Dollars

Since 1968 — Mint Mark

1964 — Mint Mark

In 1964 the mint mark was located on the rear under the claw-branch. 1964 coins had a D for Denver or no mark for Philadelphia. From 1965 – 1967 there are no mint marks. From 1968 the mint mark appears on the front under the head. If the coin was minted in Philadelphia no mark appears. Starting in 1980 the "P" for Philadelphia began appearing on coins.

John F. Kennedy half dollars took the place of Walking Liberty Silver half dollars in 1964 and are still being minted today. The Kennedy half minted in 1964 was also 90% silver. From 1965 - 1970 they contained 40% silver and then were made of 75% copper and 25% nickel starting in 1971. Starting in 2002 even though Kennedy halves were still minted in low quantities, they were not released into general circulation. Collectors could purchase them for a slight premium above face value in quantity. However these coins show up in circulation all the time.

Many newbie coin enthusiasts may not be very familiar with Kennedy half dollars.

They seldom show up in change anymore and bank tellers who receive them from their customers can't wait to get rid of the coins because no one wants to carry these large heavy pieces of metal.

Please bear in mind that these halves have lots of value. Not only can you find silver versions but error coins are somewhat easy to find as well. If the U. S. Mint stops production at some point in time, then the value of the Kennedy half will skyrocket. Keep this thought active as you search for and save these half dollars.

If I were to suggest one coin and only one to focus your attention on, it would be the Kennedy half dollar. I have had great success finding lots of silver and many error coins. Let's zero in on the error coins for now. Later I will examine the subject of silver in detail.

Just like the Roosevelt Dime and the Washington Quarters mentioned in earlier chapters, some Kennedy Half Dollars were minted on silver blanks by mistake. So what years did this occur and how do you tell if you have found one of these silver mistakes worth many thousands of dollars. Coins made on silver blanks by mistake have turned up for 1971 D and 1977 D years. These Denver minted halves are very hard to find but with a payout of over $5000 why not look for them?

A normal copper Kennedy half dollar weighs 11.34 grams. If you weigh all 71 D and 77 D coins and find one that weighs 11.50 grams you may be in luck. A coin like this will need to be certified and the specific gravity test that they will do confirms the find. You can also look for a silvery appearance but this approach is very limited and may fool you so please weigh coins for these years from the Denver Mint.

You may come across a number of plated half dollars. These are coins that someone dipped in metal so they look very new and shinny. They have no value. They can be silver or gold plated. Not to be confused with proof coins that also have a very shinny surface but came from the mint, not a chemistry lab. Proof coins are only sold in sets and encased in a plastic holder. However people open them up and spend the money inside not knowing that the numismatic value of the coin drops dramatically. When you come across a Kennedy Proof coin the letter "S" will appear above the date. Only coins minted in San Francisco were put into proof sets, except for 1964 (no mint mark appears on the proof).

Here is a picture I took of an actual "S" proof coin I found in change. Notice how the pen reflects on the surface of the coin, which has a mirror-like finish to it. Plated coins are very shinny but have a dull finish to them.

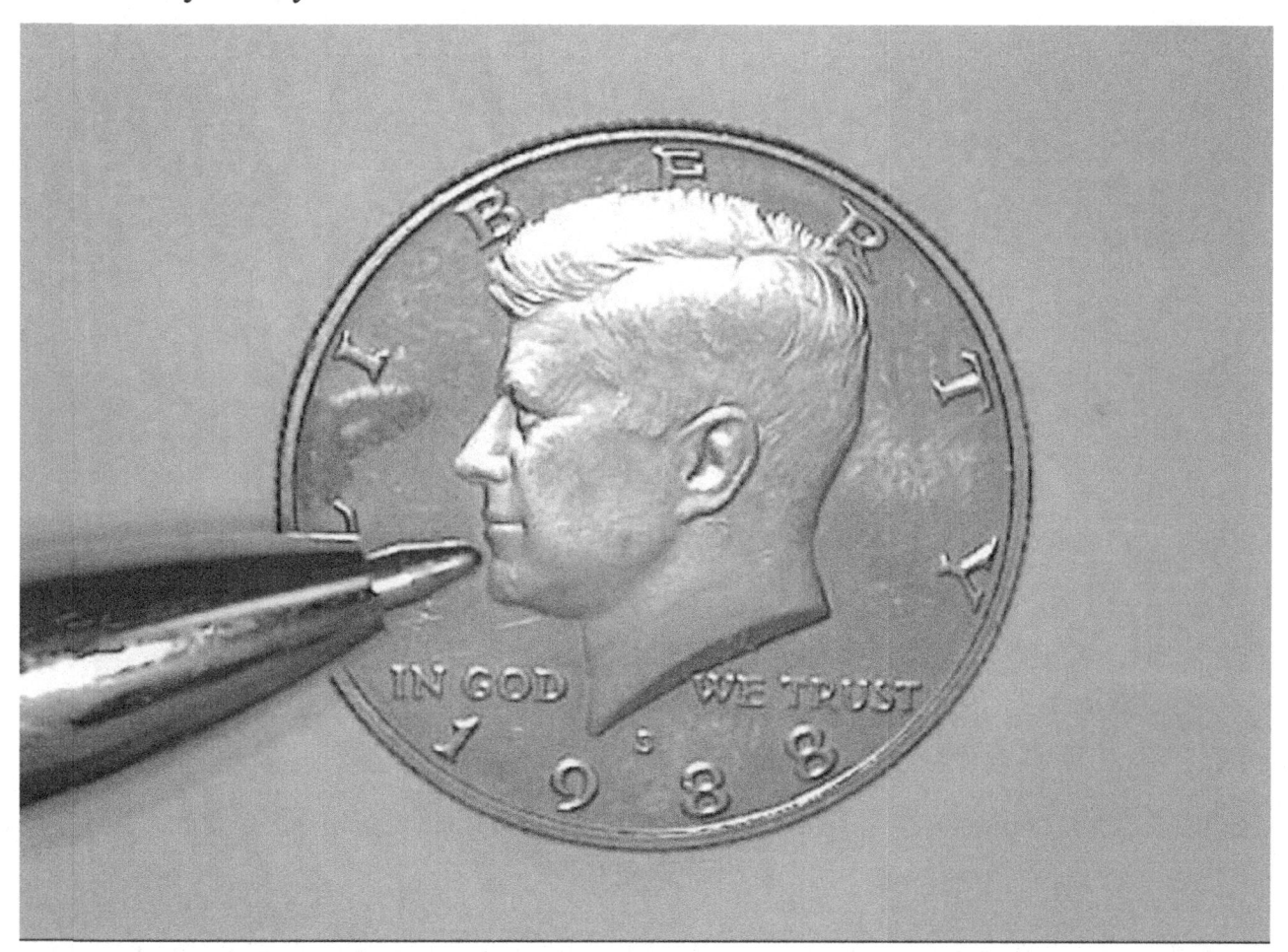

Kennedy Half Dollars are well known for having two types of errors on them: double die obverse and designer initial mistakes. Probably the best known error is the 1974 D DDO or double die obverse. These coins show very clear doubling in the phrase "In God We Trust". Look closely at the letters "RUS" as these are fairly easy to spot. I have found many of them over the years but finding one in good condition is challenging. Shown below is an example of one I found. Note the doubling on the R,U and S. This coin is very dented and it's poor condition drives the value down.

Other years that exhibit this same doubling on the front of the coin are 1971 D, 1972, 1973 D, 1977 D. The doubling on these coins is very similar to the 1974 D but not as noticeable. So if you look for them care and magnification are a must. The value for these coins varies from less than $10 to many hundreds for better condition examples.

Kennedy Half Dollars were designed by Frank Gasparro. His initials "FG" show up on the reverse of the coin just beneath the left leg of the eagle close to the body. Error coins with no letters and with one letter missing and coins with partial letters showing have been found.

Examples have been uncovered for:

1972 D - No FG

1973 D - No F

1977 D - No F

1982 P - No FG

1983 P - No FG

1989 P - No FG

No doubt there are other dates having missing letters or partial letters on them. The value for these error coins is fairly low. However one in very good condition may easily fetch over $100. Here is a picture showing the designer initials "FG" under the left leg, followed by a picture of a coin not having them:

Please keep in mind the fact that there are many variations showing up. I have found coins with no letters, only one letter – either an F only or a G only, and coins with just parts of letters showing or very thin letters. All these coin types have some value and should be saved. They are easy to find and can yield plenty of extra cash.

Coin Roll Hunting Procedure

Did you ever wonder where all the stores you do business with get the large amount of coins they always seem to have on hand in case you pay with cash and need change. Think about how many thousands of dollars worth of pennies, nickels, dimes and quarters the average Walmart must have on hand each day. What would happen if you handed the clerk a $10 bill and they did not have the loose change to pay you with when the total sale of $ 9.23 called for 77 cents in change? Has this ever happened to you?

The chances are that you have never even thought about it because they always had the correct amount of change on hand. Each day or every several days stores receive large amounts of rolled coins from their money handlers. You have seen the armored trucks deliver bills but may not have noticed the coins in rolls that they also deliver.

Smaller stores usually see the owner or manager go to the bank and come back with rolls of coins and maybe even boxes of rolled coins. A box of pennies for example weighs about 14 pounds and has $25 or 2500 pennies in it. Penny rolls come 50 cents to a roll. Much heavier boxes, such as half dollars, weigh well over 20 pounds and contain 1000 coins worth $500. Most major banks have these boxes in their vaults. However half dollar boxes usually need to be ordered.

In order to be successful with the information presented in this book you must get your hands on boxes of rolled coins. If for any reason you do not want to start big, then just ask the tellers in your bank for any rolls of coins they may have and buy them at face value.

Just to sight an example. I went into my local bank and asked the teller for any loose half dollars she had and bought about $10 worth. I could not believe my eyes when I noticed that most of them were 40% silver coins and the profit was over $50!

So how do you get boxes of rolled coins? First and foremost if you have a friendly bank and a good relationship with the bank and tellers that will give you the boxes at face value. In other words, you hand them $25 and they give you a box of 50 rolls of pennies. If your bank wants to charge you for the box or boxes I suggest you speak with the manager. Tell them you have been banking there for years and feel that they should provide you with the rolls at face value. They might argue that they pay for the boxed coins, which may or may not be true. But even if they do pay for them, it is not very much. If they insist on charging you a few dollars above face value I suggest you close your account and find another bank. If you go to a new bank and mention you will open a new account if they provide the boxes to you at face value most of the time they will work with you.

Banks want to keep you as a customer and after speaking with my bank about it they agreed to give me the boxes at face value. My best guess is that banks pay only a few dollars above face for the coin boxes. Again if you do not want to search boxes then ask the tellers for change or rolls they have in their drawer.

So several times a month I ask my bank for a box or boxes of coins. It depends upon my mood. Sometimes I like to look at pennies because of all the surprises in a box of pennies – old coins, foreign coins, new coins, error coins and the list goes on. Sometimes I ask for a box of half dollars and hand them $500. Remember, you get your money back when you deposit the coins into your account.

Another important point when it comes to dealing with your bank concerns depositing the coins so you get your money back. Most customers are unaware of the fact that your local bank has large heavy duty plastic bags used to deposit coins. They give these bags to their customers who handle lots of change. They cost less than $1 each and allow you to put your coins into the bag instead of re rolling them, which takes lots of time. So when I pick up a box of coins I always ask for the deposit bag. The bag allows you to write your name and account number on it and the amount of coin it contains.

For this to work you must keep track of how many coins you take from the box you are searching. Each time I find a keeper coin I write down what I found. For example, a 1972 penny with some doubling on it. I put the coin in a small plastic bag and label the bag # 1 to correspond with my record keeping for each coin found. This way you keep track of what the coin is and when it comes time to deposit the pennies you know how many coins are missing from the box so you can write the correct coin amount on the plastic bag. The next picture shows one type of bag. You write your name and account number and the bank tears off the tab so you have a record of the deposit and they give you a deposit receipt also.

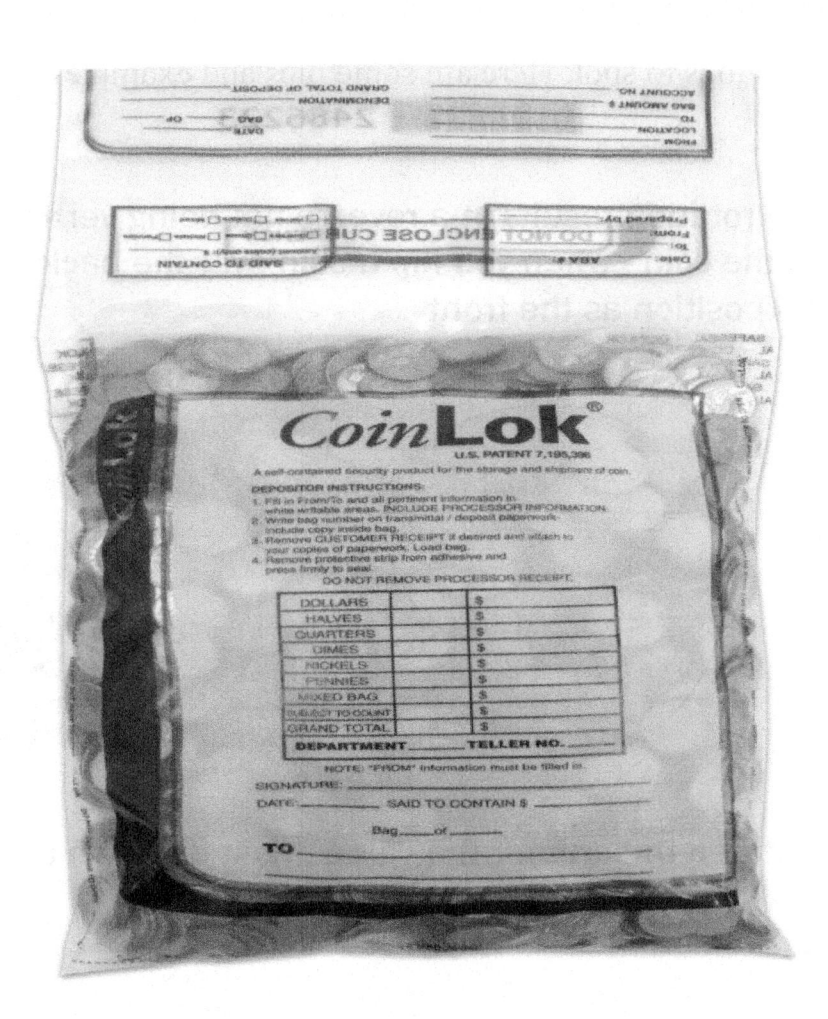

If you decide to roll the coins and put them back in the box when you are finished then care must be taken when you open the box and each roll wrapper so it can be used again. I like to pry each roll open with a small flat head screw driver by inserting it into the end of a roll and lifting the paper edge up so I can open it and pour the roll onto a large piece of cardboard or firm paper. I use one roll at a time and I check each coin against my list of errors for the coin type in question. Make sure you have your gloves on to keep your hands clean.

If I do not find anything of value in a roll I dump the coins into the plastic bag which is next to me, and hanging on my chair. The bags have a handle so it is very easy to hang them. Besides the error list I also check the coin for any abnormality, such as alignment or off center error. These types of errors have not been mentioned in this book so far because they are so obvious to spot. Here are some pics and examples:

A rotated reverse or die rotation results in a reverse not being vertical with the front or obverse of the coin - when you flip a coin over the back should be in the same vertical position as the front

The more the coin is rotated the greater the value – just flip each coin over to check for this

A clip error occurs when a new blank coin is punched from a piece of metal that already had a hole in it from previous use.

Off center strikes – coin blank was not placed in collar properly.

Double strikes – coin imprinted more than once.

Lamination error – top layer coming off or not placed on coin properly.

Broadstrike: When a perfectly centered planchet is struck out-of-collar, it expands evenly in all directions. This error can be called a "centered broadstrike". However, since the majority of broadstrikes are centered, hobbyists usually refer to it simply as a broadstrike. If the planchet is not well-centered, but the design remains complete on both faces, the error is called an "uncentered broadstrike".

Dies and Cuds: Extra metal – many variations of this error type. It occurs when the die breaks and extra metal is placed on the coin.

One of the best web sites ever developed on error coins is listed below:
http://www.error-ref.com/

This site lists every possible error by name and provides detailed pictures. It is designed for the advanced collector, but worth taking a look at and having as a reference.

Once you look at this site you realize that the error topic in and of itself can become a life time pursuit.

Keep in mind the fact that when you look at coins you need very good lighting and must maintain good posture. Bring the coin up to you. Do not bend over to look at coins. The more light you have and the more magnification the better the results.

Please remember that this is a number's and time game. The more time you spend on this the better you get and the more valuable coins you find. Years ago when I first started looking at rolls of coins I seldom found anything of value. The reason was due to my inexperience at this. My eyes were not trained and I had a really hard time deciding what I was looking at but as time went by I became really good at it and can go through a box of coins rapidly and with good results. Practice makes perfect.

Please never mention to the bank tellers what you are looking for. They are not stupid and will quickly realize what coins have value if you tell them. I never tell the tellers anything. I might mention that I look for error coins and when they ask which ones I tell them that there are over 200 errors I look for and then end the conversation.

Not shown in the following picture is a box of Half Dollars which is $500 and weighs over 20 pounds. All coins in these boxes are rolled and contain 50 coins per roll.

Finding Silver

This is my favorite subject of all and if you do nothing else but look for silver coins then this in and of itself will be worthwhile. I have found thousands of dollars worth of silver over the years and here is how I do it. On average you have to look at around $10,000 worth of coins to find one silver coin. With these odds it is a complete waste of time to just look through change unless you focus on nickels and half dollars. On average I find one silver nickel per box of $100 in nickels or 2000 coins weighing 22 pounds. This may seem like a small result but I am also looking for error coins as well. The silver nickels are the war time ones minted from mid1942 – 1945.

However, as much fun as nickel hunting is I prefer looking for silver half dollars. Here is where the real gold is. You can find lots of silver half dollars per box of coins. A box of halves has 1000 coins in it and cost $500. Some boxes have no silver and some have lots of silver. I have found as many as 12 silver coins in one box of halves. If you are just looking for silver then you can go through a box in just a few minutes. Remember 1964 halves are 90% silver. Do not look for silvery coins, look at the dates.

Coins minted from 1965 – 1970 are 40% silver. The reason these coins are fairly easy to find is due to two main factors. Very few people search through Kennedy Half Dollar rolls because they do not want to spend $500 or are unaware that you can still get half dollars in change from your bank. But the principle reason is due to the incredible number of silver coins minted.

In 1964 a total of 433,460,212 90% silver coins were minted and released into change. That's almost one half billion coins. Then from 1965 – 1970 another billion coins containing 40% silver were minted and released. So my question is where are all these coins now? Yes many are hoarded by collectors but do you think anyone can find lots of them by looking through half dollar rolls? You certainly can! Here is a picture of a set of silver coins I found using the methods listed in this book. This one sale brought in well over $200. All these coins are 40% silver Kennedy half dollars.

It's as simple as looking at the dates on each half dollar. If it says 1964 then you have found a 90% silver coin. I have found lots of them and some are so dirty that they do not look like silver. If the date is 1965 – 1970 then you have found a 40% silver coin.

It is easy to check the melt value of the coin by looking at the coinflation web site mentioned earlier. And for coins that are in really good condition they may be worth more than their silver content is.

A final tip and this one pays off big. Whenever I go to the supermarket I check the Coinstar machine bin where rejected coins fall. Believe or not silver coins usually fall into the reject bin. The machine does not like them and customers just leave them there. I have found lots of silver dimes and quarters this way.

Determining Coin Values

The value of a coin is based upon one main factor and only one: what someone is willing to pay for it! This may seem very simplistic but when you think about a rare painting what actually are you getting for your money? You get some canvas and paint and a border around it. With a coin you get a small piece of metal with a date and some images on it. The value has nothing to do with the date or how old it is, it has nothing to do with what metal it is made of (unless it is gold or the wrong metal) or really what condition it is in. The price it sells for is based upon demand and interest only. This rule covers most of the coins listed in this book.

There are very rare coins with low mintage that sell for very little money because the interest is not there. I have pennies that are hundreds of years old and very rare but worth very little. On the other hand a 1943 D copper penny sold for almost 2 million dollars. Why? It is based upon interest. Collectors want certain types of coins and the date or mintage and condition are not always critical factors. With respect to the 1943 D copper penny, only one of these coins has ever been found, and this added to its value but the demand and interest in the coin drove the price up. If Elvis Presley owned a car and it sold for $2 million and you owned the exact same type car and your car sold for $20000, what happened?

I am sure you see the point here. I am not saying that condition and rarity are not important, it is. But the main factor is demand. That being said, coin books that show value are giving you a very rough estimate only. The only way to determine worth is to see what identical coins are selling for.

Let's divide coins into two groups. The first group is for coins that do not have lots of value. The second group is for coins worth thousands. Where is the dividing point here? Is it $500, $1000, $10000. I cannot answer this. If you consider a coin to be very valuable and want to get top dollar for it you must first determine:

- Is the coin real vs a fake? Has it been verified by a reputable grading company?
- What do similar coins sell for?
- Do coins like these sell online at eBay or do they sell through top auction companies like Heritage, for example.

This process is identical to art work. First the art is verified. Then the auction house estimates value and puts it up for sale and might set a minimum price before it can be purchased. Unless the bidding reaches the minimum the painting will not be sold to anyone.

When you find a coin that you consider to be of value first go online to sites like eBay and see what similar coins are selling for. This is a good starting point. Look closely at the condition and description so you can compare your coin to it. Next post pictures of your coin on forums mentioned in this book and see what the experts have to say. Try to determine if the coin is the real error in question and try to determine condition. Value their opinions but don't take them to the bank. Show it to the local coin club and get their view also. Do not show it to any local coin stores.

For a coin worth thousands you must have it verified by a major grading company and then sold by a reputable auction house. For one worth hundreds you should sell it yourself. I would not spend any money having a coin graded unless it was worth well over $100.

Dealing with a grading company is a very simple procedure. Most of the work can be done online but I prefer calling them first and finding out the procedure for sending in a coin for identification and grading. The fee for this is minimal and is necessary. No one will pay for a valuable coin that has not been certified. Before going to this expense I suggest you contact the auction houses and find out what their policy is for submitting a coin for sale. They may have you send the coin to them and have it graded for you. Policies change all the time so call first.

Auction companies to consider:

While there are more than two I suggest these because I feel you will get the best sale price for your coins by dealing with them.

- Heritage is the largest of them all and has offices all over the world and in many American cities:

    Ha.com

    Contact them at 877-HERITAGE (437-4824) or Bid@HA.com

- Stack's and Bowers is another great one to consider and is worldwide.

    http://www.stacksbowers.com

    1 800 458 4646

    info@stacksbowers.com

Grading companies to consider:

There are 4 well known ones which I will list here but the first one mentioned is the preferred choice:

- The Professional Coin Grading Service (PCGS)
- The Numismatic Guaranty Corporation (NGC)
- Independent Coin Graders (ICG)
- ANACS

    The Professional Coin Grading Service:

    PCGS.com

    1 800 447 8848

    The Numismatic Guaranty Corporation

    www.NGCcoin.com

    1 800 NGC-COIN

    Independent Coin Graders

    ICGCoin.com

    1 877 221 4424

    ANACS

    Anacs.com

    1 800 888 1861

Let's look at an example for one of the error coins mentioned in this book: 1974 D DDO (Double Die Obverse) Kennedy Half Dollar. I found this coin listed on eBay. See the picture below. Notice how the coin has been graded by PCGS and the condition of the coin is listed as MS64 or Mint State 64. This coin is selling for $75 and another similar one in slightly better condition is going for $195 on eBay. When a coin is graded the company doing the assessment puts the coin in a plastic container and labels it as the picture shows. The seller spent the $30-40 to have the coin graded and verified in an attempt to get a high price for the coin but you have to question whether or not it was worth it. After paying eBay fees and the grading fee the profit is only about $30. I would have asked more than $75 for this coin.

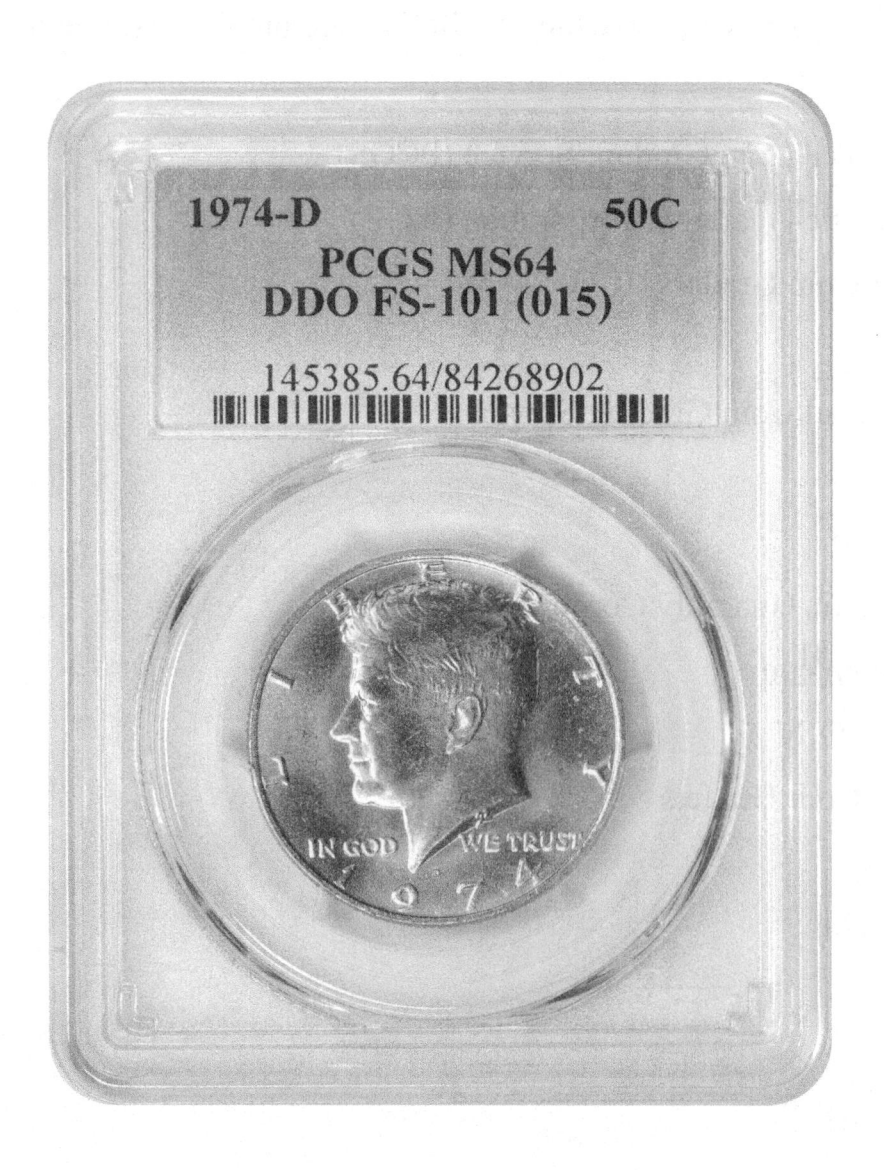

Selling Coins

In the last chapter eBay and auction houses were mentioned with respect to selling. There are many ways to sell a coin. If you belong to a local coin club, for example, auctioning or selling at a meeting may bring good results. However, I have found that eBay is the easiest, fastest and most productive way to sell coins. Coins worth thousands should be auctioned, as stated.

Over a many year period I have sold thousands of dollars worth of coins on eBay and have always gotten a high price for them. If you are not an eBay seller I strongly suggest you register now and start selling so you gain some experience. Sell anything you can get your hands on in order to get your feet wet. Amazon is not a good platform for selling coins.

A great way to gain experience is to follow auctions on eBay. Watch what identical coins are selling for and try to gain insight as to why some coins sell for more money even though they are identical.

If you are not familiar with using eBay for selling I'm going to provide some basic information here for you. Also, my email address is linked in the beginning and end of this book so feel free to contact me if you need help.

Setting Up PayPal and eBay Accounts

PayPal

Paypal.com

Every day around the world, millions of people use PayPal to make purchases online. It's the easiest, safest and most trusted way for you to accept payments for your eBay auctions. I've been a satisfied PayPal customer for over 15 years. Set up a PayPal Business account and pay no monthly fees when you select the PayPal Payments Standard option. With a PayPal business account, you can also benefit from reduced transaction fees. PayPal has great phone support; call if you ever need help with your account:

    1-888-221-1161

    1-402-935-2050 (if calling from outside the U.S.)

    4:00 A.M. to 10:00 P.M. Pacific Time Monday through Friday

    6:00 A.M. to 8:00 P.M. Pacific Time Saturday and Sunday

Please note that hours of operation may vary on holidays.

Ebay

eBay.com

On the top of the eBay homepage, click where it says register, and then click **"start a business account"**. A business account has several advantages over a personal account, such as giving you a more professional presence as an eBay seller. It'll pay for itself many times over. There is no fee to register a business account. As with PayPal, eBay has excellent customer support. Even if you aren't registered with eBay, phone support at 1-866-540-3229 is available to you from 5:00 A.M. to 10:00 P.M. Pacific Time, seven days a week. eBay's Seller Information Center has everything you need to get started with selling on eBay as quickly as possible. Please review it before listing your first auction.

Getting The Best Auction Results

Why does one item on eBay sell for $20.00, while the same in a different auction sells for $35.00 or more? There are several possible explanations for this significant difference in sales results:

- ✔ Auction listed to end when most people aren't using eBay, such as 2 A. M.
- ✔ Poor pictures—too large, too small, containing insufficient detail or taking too long to load
- ✔ Poor feedback from customers
- ✔ Poorly-worded description

- ✔ Item listed in wrong category
- ✔ Starting price too high—the leading cause of auction failure!

In the sections that follow, I'll address these issues so you can get the best results from your auctions.

Step One: The Photograph

Any basic digital camera with a macro function (close-up mode) will work fine. If you're selling errors, a USB hand held digital microscope is an inexpensive, easy-to-use tool to capture clear, close-up photos of them. A Celestron 44302 Deluxe Hand-held Digital Microscope 2MP is a good example as mentioned earlier.

For a $45.00 investment on Amazon.com, this microscope captures brilliant clarity and fine details beyond the technical capabilities of my regular digital camera. Good photos can help increase your bids and final values.

You can also use stock photos in your eBay ad. You must mention that the image you use is not the actual picture of the coin.

Here are some tips for taking the best photographs:

1. Take five opaque (non-white) empty milk gallon jugs and cut the bottoms off straight at one, two, three, four and five inches below the handle.
2. Place the coins on a dark-colored towel or sheet of paper placed on a table. Place the jug so the opening is on top and the cut-out section is over the items.
3. Take pictures outdoors and in sunlight, but stand under a porch roof or canopy so you're not standing directly in the sun's rays.
4. Place the camera lens over the milk jug opening.
5. Experiment with different light settings on your camera.
6. Experiment with the macro mode to get the camera into close focus and produce super-magnified results.

7. Always take three to four pictures of each item(s) so you can pick the one(s) that looks best.
8. If you need to take a picture of a large number of coins go outside under your porch and place the money on a dark-colored towel or sheet of paper. Zoom the camera into close focus and use the setting on your camera for taking standard pictures. The camera needs to be held steady, so use a tripod.

The Category

Picking the best category is important. Ebay has categories for U.S. Money types, such as half dollars – Kennedy and for error coins. If you are selling an item worth $25 or more picking two categories can work to your advantage. The extra fee is worth the investment. Always check similar coins to see what categories they are listed under.

The Title

After selecting a category or categories, the Create your listing page appears. At the top, click Switch to "form with more choices" and then click Continue. Write a descriptive title of the item in 80 characters or less. Good titles will drive traffic to your auction listings. Since eBay users see titles first after searching for items, your titles must stand out from the crowd. The more visible your listing, the more money you'll make. Good titles also help users find your auctions more easily. Always take the time to ensure that your titles are as descriptive and appealing as possible. Titles must have strong key words, such as error, unc (if it is uncirculated), rare, etc... These key words must be accurate and describe the coin you are selling.

Here is a free tool that allows you to create great titles and it provides other useful information. It is very easy to use. It is called Title Builder:

http://www.title-builder.com/

The Picture

As of this writing, eBay allows you to upload up to 12 pictures for free. Click Add pictures and on the Standard tab, select your pictures to upload. After uploading, click the Trash icon to remove any unwanted photos on the page. When viewers of your auction listing move their mouse over the pictures, a small section is magnified to display additional detail. This feature is included at no additional cost. The more pictures you upload, the better the results. Only use pictures that are clear and have no light reflecting back from them. If you know HTML and how to upload pictures to a web server, you can include free pictures in your description.

The Description

The item description is the section where many sellers sabotage their auction listings. Keep it brief and to the point! If the picture you use is a stock photo and not an actual picture of the coin, you must mention this in the description. Use color and a large font. I've found that a simple description such as this one, works especially well:

Beautiful Kennedy Half Dollar Error Coin

Mint Condition – Check Picture Out For Details
I found this looking through change

Auction or Fixed Price?

The auction starting price is another area where many eBay sellers make big mistakes. As a general rule of thumb, click the Online Auction tab and set your starting price at 99 cents. I always start my auctions at 99 cents. At this price, your auction will attract attention and end up with more bids. Because the demand for coins is high, the auction will always bid up to a good final price.

To summarize, buyers enjoy bidding on items priced low. The higher your starting price, the less likely you are to get bids. Notice how eBay auctions with high starting prices usually have no bids and never sell. Auctions with low starting prices tend to attract lots of bids. Always remember to use a pricing strategy that protects you from loss and fits your specific item.

Always select 7 days for the auction duration, and always select Schedule start time. You'll have additional time to make changes as needed and ensure that your auction looks good. Always set your auctions to start on Sunday at 5 to 6 P.M. Pacific Standard Time. This is very important for getting the best results. The only exception is when special events, such as sports on television, occur on Sunday night, the ending time for your auction. If people are watching TV, odds are they won't be watching your auction.

Make sure to leave PayPal selected as your payment method.

Shipping

Always charge a flat fee for shipping. Never overcharge for shipping. Expensive items should be insured. First class mail works best. Make sure your item is sandwiched between cardboard so it is protected. A coin sent by itself – no packing around it, can actually slip out of an envelope when the post office sends it through a reader. The reader only allows a certain thickness and the coin gets pressed out of the envelope. Take the coin to the window and have the letter stamped by the clerk so it does not have to be processed.

Buyer Requirements

Use Buyer Requirements to block certain buyers from bidding on or purchasing your items. I make no changes in this section, but you have the option to make changes of your own.

Return Policy

You won't get many (if any) returns, but give buyers confidence in you by accepting them. Click Change your return policy and then click Returns Accepted. I make no other changes in this section, but as with Buyer Requirements, you can make changes to fit your specific requirements.

Going Live With Your Auction

Once you're finished, preview your auction and then list it. Go back and look at it several times to make sure it looks right. You've plenty of time to make changes since you've scheduled your listing to appear at a later date.

Once your auction goes live, you must watch it, check your email for customer questions, and reply promptly to them. What if no one bids on it? You can always list it again. What if it only gets one bid? Are you forced to sell it for 99 cents? You can cancel the auction just before it ends but this is not a good practice.

Once it ends, you should sell it to the highest bidder. Otherwise, you risk getting negative feedback on your selling record.

Customer Service

When dealing with eBay buyers, always be friendly and give them the benefit of the doubt. If they're unhappy with your product, do whatever it takes to make them feel better about doing business with you. Never argue over money. As you build up a good reputation and get lots of positive feedback, your auctions will become more and more successful.

I've only covered the basics here regarding PayPal and eBay. But you have enough information to get started and make some money.

Quick Start Guide

In this section I would like to organize the information presented so you have a very useful-handy reference to follow when you look for coins of value. For each coin denomination I created a list. Let's start with pennies:

Lincoln Pennies:

1943, 1943 D, 1943 S Copper Penny   Copper vs Steel – Look for Copper Colored Penny (An S 1943 copper penny was recently found)

1964 Penny With Special Finish – Look For Very Shinny Coin

1969 S DDO – Look for strong doubling on the front letters

1970 S Large Date DDO – Look for doubling in Motto

1970 S Small Date – Not an error but hard so keep

1972 DDO – Doubling on front – many varieties so check all letters

1982 DDR – Very rare coin doubling on back letters

1983 Copper Penny – Weigh all 1983 coins 3.1 grams is rare copper coin

1983 Extra Letters in Motto – Extra "G"

1983 DDR – Doubling letters on back of coin

1984 DDO – Doubling on ear and chin

1988 & 1988 D - Bold designer initials **"FG"**

1992 & 1992 D - Close "AM"

1995 DDO – Doubling on front letters

1999 – AM far apart instead of close

Jefferson Nickels:

1942 – 1945   War nickels had 35 % silver in them (1942 silver nickels have a large "P" above the dome or a large S). 1942 D coins have no silver.

1942 P and S coins have silver in them

1943 – 1945 D,P and S coins all have silver in them

1939 DDR – 2 types: one has strong doubling on letters "Of America, United States, and Cents" This type is not worth as much as the one with doubling on the word "Monticello"

1943 DDO – Doubling on front letters

1943 3/2 – The number 3 sits over a number 2

1945 DDR – The word "Monticello" on the back has doubling

1946 DDO – The date and the word "Liberty" have doubling

1954 DDR – The words "Pluribus" and Unum" have doubling

1956 D, 1959 D, 1962 D, 1964 D all have some doubling on the reverse

2004 DDO – Doubling on the date and word "Trust"

2005 D – The buffalo has a spear running through it (reverse side)

Roosevelt Dimes:

1965 and 1966 - Some dimes were minted on silver blanks by mistake silver coins weigh 2.5 grams compared to 2.27 grams for normal dimes

1967 DDO – Look for doubling in the motto

1968 – The date and letters have doubling

1970 DDR – Look for strong doubling on the reverse side

1970 D DDR – Look for doubling in the words "United States"

1974 D – Look for the head showing up on the back side (counter clash)

1982 – Look for coins with no "P" mint mark – Coin has date only on it

Washington Quarters:

1965 & 1968 S Silver coins by mistake – Silver weighs 6.25 grams vs 5.67

1965, 1967, 1970-D, 1979 – Coins minted on wrong stock resulting in coins made on very thin metal – skinny as a dime. May be true for other years as well.

1965 DDO – Doubling on motto and word "Liberty" on reverse

1968 D DDR – Doubling on reverse (Bold doubling)

1970 D DDO – Doubling on motto and date on front

1971 DDR – Doubling on words "United States"

1971 D DDR – Doubling in the phrase "United States of America"

1976 D DDO – Doubling on reverse the word "Liberty" (Strong doubling)

1999 P & D – Under the name Caesar Rodney a second Rodney appears

2004 D – Extra corn leaf – one is high, the other low – 2 types

2009 – Extra letters under name Duke Ellington – extra "ELL"

Kennedy Halves:

1964 – 90% silver

1965 – 1970 40% silver

1976 "S" – 90% silver coins put into special sets but may show up in change

(Weigh all 1976 S coins found – a silver coin weighs 11.50 grams)

1971 D & 1977 D Minted on silver blank by mistake 11.5 grams for silver

                                                                                          11.34 for non silver

1974 D DDO – Doubling: look at letters "RUS" - Same for the following:

1971 D DDO

1972 DDO

1973 D DDO

1977 D DDO

1972 D – No FG

1973 D – No F

1977 D – No F

1982 P – No FG

1983 P – No FG

Conclusion and Summary

Thank you for taking this journey with me into the world of error and silver coins. It was designed to help beginners get started and I hope it achieves this objective. For many decades I have reaped the rewards of my knowledge and experience as it relates to coins and eBay and what is so great about this methodology is that you can use it to your advantage whenever you are in the mood to make some quick money or find some great coins for collecting.

The extra money I made finding silver and error coins over the years came in handy on many an occasion and I know that if you stick with this system, it will pay off. Please, if you are new to this be patient with yourself. I guarantee that over time so will be amazed at how good you will become by trial and error. Practice makes perfect.

Please email me at any time. My email address is storm@ctaz.com . Please check out my other books. They contain lots of goodies.

Web Links Mentioned:

Celestron Digital Microscope

Search Amazon For: "Celestron 44302 Deluxe Handheld Digital USB Microscope"
Actual link:
https://www.amazon.com/Celestron-Handheld-Digital-Microscope-Capture/dp/B004QF0A1Y/ref=sr_1_7?s=electronics&ie=UTF8&qid=1507072142&sr=1-7&keywords=celestron+digital+microscope

Gram Scale (American Weigh Scales)

Search Amazon For: "American Weigh Scales AWS-600-BLK Digital Personal Nutrition Scale"

Actual Link:

https://www.amazon.com/American-Weigh-Scales-AWS-600-BLK-Nutrition/dp/B000O37TDO/ref=sr_1_1?s=home-garden&ie=UTF8&qid=1507073054&sr=1-1&keywords=american+weigh+gram+scale

Nitrile Gloves (Dynarez)

Search Amazon For: "Dynarex 2511 SafeTouch Nitrile Exam Gloves"

Actual Link:

https://www.amazon.com/Dynarex-2513-SafeTouch-Nitrile-Non-Latex/dp/B01LVTVK57/ref=sr_1_1?s=home-garden&ie=UTF8&qid=1507073175&sr=1-1&keywords=nitrile+gloves+dynarex

Magnified Loupe (Gadgetscollection)

Search eBay For:"20x Lighted LED Illuminated Jewelry Eye Loupe Magnifier Magnifying Glass Lens"

Actual Link:

https://www.ebay.com/itm/20x-Lighted-LED-Illuminated-Jewelry-Eye-Loupe-Magnifier-Magnifying-Glass-Lens-/371977293780?hash=item569b930fd4:g:Fd8AAOSw1~JZOxxi

Coin Clubs:

www.money.org This website has links to local coin clubs

Coin Forums:

http://www.coincommunity.com/dictionary/

https://www.cointalk.com/forums/

www.Coinpeople.com

Melt Value – Silver & Gold

http://www.coinflation.com/silver_coin_values.html

Web Link For Error Coins:

http://www.error-ref.com/

Web Link For Auction Houses:

Ha.com

http://www.stacksbowers.com

Grading Companies To Consider:

PCGS.com

NGCCoin.com

ICGCoin.com

Anacs.com

Web Site That Helps Build Your Online Title – For eBay & Other Sites

http://www.title-builder.com/

Made in the USA
Monee, IL
20 June 2024